Marvel Studios' Doctor Strange

Based on the Screenplay by
Jon Spaihts, Scott Derrickson, and C. Robert Cargill
Story by Stan Lee and Steve Ditko

Produced by Kevin Feige, p.g.a.
Directed by Scott Derrickson

Level 3

Retold by Mary Tomalin

Series Editors: Andy Hopkins and Jocelyn Potter

T0345464

Pearson Education Limited

KAO Two

KAO Park, Harlow,

Essex, CM17 9NA, England

and Associated Companies throughout the world.

ISBN: 978-1-2923-4748-6

This edition first published by Pearson Education Ltd 2018

1 3 5 7 9 10 8 6 4 2

Set in 9pt/14pt Xenois Slab Pro

Printed by Neografia, Slovakia

Published by Pearson Education Limited

For a complete list of the titles available in the Pearson English Readers series, visit
www.pearsonenglishreaders.com.
Alternatively, write to your local Pearson Education office or
to Pearson English Readers Marketing Department,
Pearson Education, KAO Two, KAO Park, Harlow, Essex, CM17 9NA

Contents

In This Story

Dr. Stephen Strange

He is a top surgeon. He is very intelligent, but he is also proud and selfish. His work is very important to him. He works with another surgeon, Dr. Christine Palmer, in a New York hospital. Palmer was Strange's girlfriend.

The Ancient One

She is a very powerful sorcerer. There have been "Ancient Ones" for thousands of years. She protects the Earth against dangerous, magical powers. She lives in a Sanctum in Kamar-Taj. She guides and teaches sorcerers.

Mordo

Mordo is a master sorcerer who works closely with the Ancient One in Kamar-Taj. He teaches his skills to student sorcerers. He believes very strongly in the Ancient One, and her fight to defend the Earth.

Wong

Wong is also a master sorcerer at the Kamar-Taj Sanctum. Kamar-Taj has a large library of books about magic, and Wong is the librarian there. He believes in the fight to protect the Earth.

Kaecilius and the Zealots

Kaecilius was a master sorcerer in Kamar-Taj, but left with the Zealots—a group of unhappy sorcerers. He now works with dark powers that want to destroy the Sanctums and the Earth.

Magical weapons

Sorcerers can catch and hit people with **energy whips**, thin lines of energy. These are made using **sling rings**. With sling rings, sorcerers can travel through the Multiverse. Sorcerers use their hands to make **Space Shards**—long, pointed knives of energy.

Magical relics

"Relics" have very strong powers. Wearing the **Cloak of Levitation**, a sorcerer can fly. This long coat also helps a sorcerer in danger. In the **Vaulting Boots of Valtorr**, a sorcerer can climb walls, jump very high, and move in the air.

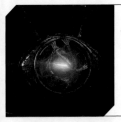

The Eye of Agamotto

This relic is passed between the most important sorcerers and holds the Time Stone. Using its great power, skilled sorcerers can change time. They can stop it and move it back. They can even make new timelines and new realities.

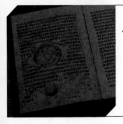

The Book of Cagliostro

Cagliostro wrote this old book of powerful spells after he studied the Eye of Agamotto. The spells help skilled sorcerers use the Eye, but many of them are very dangerous. The book is kept in the Ancient One's private library in Kamar-Taj.

Introduction

◆━━━━━━━━━━━━━━━━━━━━━━━━━━━━━◆

"The language of the mystic arts is very old," the Ancient One said. "Sorcerers called this language 'spells.'"

She and Strange were on their knees. Waving her arms, the Ancient One drew a line of bright orange energy in the air. She turned the line, and it became a circle. A square appeared around the circle, and then smaller circles appeared.

"We use energy that comes from other parts of the Multiverse," she said. "We use this energy to cast spells. We also use it to make weapons."

When Dr. Stephen Strange, one of the world's best surgeons, has a terrible car accident, his life changes completely. His hands are badly damaged in the accident, and he cannot work as a surgeon again. Strange thinks that his life is finished. Then, he learns about a place called Kamar-Taj, in Nepal. Maybe this place can help him. In Kamar-Taj, he meets a great sorcerer called the Ancient One.

"You only see a part of the world, not the complete picture," she tells him. Strange learns that magic is real. The Ancient One teaches Strange to cast spells. Slowly, he becomes a powerful sorcerer. He also learns the deeper secrets of the universe. There are living things in other parts of the universe that want to destroy the Earth. The Ancient One and her sorcerers protect the world from attack. And now, the world is in great danger. Strange must decide. Will he fight with the Ancient One and defend the Earth?

The film, *Marvel Studios' Doctor Strange*, was made in 2016 and was a big success all over the world. Three of the main actors sound American, but they are British. Benedict Cumberbatch plays Doctor Strange, and Tilda Swinton plays the Ancient One. Chiwetel Ejiofor plays the sorcerer Mordo. *Doctor Strange* is the fourteenth movie in the Marvel Cinematic Universe. In this imaginary universe, men and women with special powers fight against their enemies, good against bad. The stories often happen in our world. Doctor Strange appears in three other movies: *Marvel Studios'*

Thor: Ragnarok, *Marvel Studios' Avengers: Infinity War*, and *Marvel Studios' Avengers: Endgame*. There will be a second film about Doctor Strange, *Marvel Studios' Doctor Strange in the Multiverse of Madness* (2022).

People have always been interested in magic. It is a very special power. It can do things that don't seem possible. For thousands of years, people believed in magic. Today, science tells us that it does not exist. There are only the natural laws of the universe.

But something can be "magic" until we understand it. Can the mind help the body to repair itself? Scientists think that this is possible. In *Doctor Strange*, a man has had an accident, and cannot walk. He goes to Kamar-Taj. With the use of magic, he learns to walk again.

There are many books and movies about magic. *Doctor Strange* is another great story about its power.

Prologue: Kamar-Taj, Kathmandu

The sorcerer Kaecilius and a group of his Zealots walked into the dark library of Kamar-Taj. Kaecilius was a tall, strong man, with a face that wasn't kind. His long hair was tied at the back. Now, he looked around the library, remembering it from many years ago. It had the largest number of books about magic in the world, and he knew many of them well. He was ready, at last, to read a very special book.

The librarian and the other sorcerers in the library saw the group. They knew Kaecilius. They immediately cast spells to protect themselves. But Kaecilius was too quick and powerful for them. He and his group had Space Shards that could cut through everything. They used energy whips that came from the sling rings on their fingers. The librarian and the other sorcerers were quickly killed.

Kaecilius walked to the Ancient One's shelf. There, the *Book of Cagliostro* was waiting for him. It was one of the greatest books about magic in the world, with spells that were thousands of years old. Kaecilius knew some

It looked like a mirror that was broken into a thousand pieces—the Mirror Dimension.

of them already. He wanted to learn one very dangerous spell. He knew that he was ready for it. He found the pages in the book. Reading the spell, he could feel the power in it. He pulled the pages out and dropped the book on the floor.

"Master Kaecilius," a woman's voice said. "If you use that spell, you will be very sorry."

He knew the woman well. Turning around, he saw her at the door of the library. She wore a yellow robe, and her face was covered. He waved his arms, and a portal opened. He and his Zealots ran through it and out onto a London street. They ran along the sidewalk.

She won't follow us, Kaecilius thought.

He was wrong. Suddenly, a wall appeared in front of them. It looked like a mirror that was broken into a thousand pieces—the Mirror Dimension. They couldn't pass it. When they turned around, the woman was walking toward them.

She wants all the power, Kaecilius thought angrily. *But that is going to change.*

The woman waved her arms. The buildings turned on their sides until they were below Kaecilius's feet. The group fell but got up again. The woman made another movement with her arms, and parts of the buildings began to spin. Some of the Zealots were caught in them and killed. The other Zealots ran toward the woman. She threw circles of energy at them. Some fell down. She fought with the others, using both magical power and martial arts. Then, she turned the buildings upside down, and now Kaecilius and his group were hanging on to an upside-down building.

Kaecilius had the pages from the book and didn't want to fight the woman. He pointed down and opened another portal. The Zealots jumped through it and out of the Mirror Dimension, and he followed them. The Mirror Dimension disappeared.

The woman stopped the spell, and the buildings moved back to their usual position. She returned from the Mirror Dimension to the real world and uncovered her head. Some people looked twice at her shaven head and her yellow robe, but then they looked away. This was London.

Kaecilius must not use that spell, she thought.

Dr. Stephen Strange Has an Accident

It was an ordinary day for Dr. Stephen Strange. He was operating on a patient with a very unusual problem. While he worked, he listened to pop music. He was the best in the world at his job, and some students were watching. He knew everything about the body. He could do the most difficult operations, and his hands never shook.

The operation was almost finished when Strange saw Dr. Christine Palmer through the window of the operating room. For a short time, she was Strange's girlfriend. Now they were friends, and both worked as surgeons. He finished his work and left the room.

"I'd like you to work with me when I have difficult patients," Christine said.

"I can't do that. *My* work is too important," Strange replied.

"Yes, you're right. We only *save lives* in *my* job. There are no T.V. interviews," Christine said.

"I'm speaking tonight at an important dinner. Come with me," Strange said softly.

She refused.

"When we were together, you loved going to those things. We had fun," he said.

"No," she laughed. "*You* had fun. They weren't about us. They were about *you*."

"Not *only* about me."

"Stephen," she said, still smiling, but sad at the same time, "*everything* is about you."

And she walked away.

Strange's apartment was high above the city of New York and covered a complete floor. He took some time to get ready for the dinner. He shaved, looking at himself in the mirror. *I look good,* he thought. *But I always look good*. He chose one of his expensive watches and put it on. Then, he left his apartment, and drove fast out of the city.

He was outside New York on a road high above the Hudson River when a nurse, Billy, called.

"We have a thirty-five-year-old soldier who broke his lower back in an accident," Billy said.

"Too ordinary," Strange said.

Billy told him about another patient.

"That sounds interesting," he said.

Billy sent pictures to Strange's phone, and the doctor looked at them. As he was passing another car, he looked at the pictures again. This was a mistake. His car hit the other car, went off the road, and hit a tree. It dropped a long way and fell upside down into the Hudson River.

When Strange woke up, he was in a hospital bed. Christine was there.

"Hey," she said softly. "It's O.K. It's going to be O.K."

What day was it? He didn't know. His eyes began to see more clearly. He looked at her, then down the bed. There were thin pieces of metal all over his hands. Clearly, the damage to them was terrible.

"What did the surgeon do?" he asked slowly.

Christine explained. Strange wasn't found immediately. When he *was* found, he was taken to the hospital very fast. But it was too late for his hands—they were very badly damaged.

"What did the surgeon do?" he asked again. His hands were so important to him. Without them, he was nothing.

Christine told him about the operation. "You were on the table for eleven hours. They did the best that they could do."

He didn't agree.

Two weeks later, Strange was finally able to try using his hands. They shook when he held them up.

"No!" he said. He couldn't believe it. "You've destroyed me," he told his surgeon.

He went to all the best doctors, but they couldn't help. He had a second operation and did hours and hours of hand exercises. But his hands still shook all the time.

Then, a hospital nurse told him about a patient called Jonathan Pangborn.

"He had a factory accident and broke his back," the nurse said. "He couldn't use his legs. Then, a few years later, he walked past me on the street."

"Walked?"

"Yes, he walked."

Strange knew that wasn't possible. But he asked for more information about Pangborn. While he waited for the information, he did the exercises. Nothing helped. At the end of a month, he still couldn't shave his face, and he could only write his name with difficulty. He talked to all the world's top surgeons. They couldn't help.

Strange felt terrible. He wasn't looking after himself well. His hair was longer. He couldn't shave, so he had a beard and a mustache. He didn't think about his clothes. Only one thing was important to him—his work. And he couldn't do it because of his hands. He had another problem now, too. Operations were very expensive, and all his money was gone.

"Maybe it's time to stop looking for help," Christine said when she visited him.

"No," he said. "I *can't* stop! I'm not getting better!"

"Stephen, you won't succeed."

"Life without my work ...," he said.

"... is still life," said Christine. "This isn't the end. You can find meaning in other things."

"Like what? Like *you?*" he said angrily.

That hurt her. "You should say sorry," she said.

"No, you should leave," he shouted.

"Fine," she said unhappily. "I can't watch you do this."

"Is it too difficult for you?"

"Yes, it is," said Christine. "I feel so sad, seeing you like this."

"No! *Don't* feel sorry for me!"

Christine looked at him sadly. "Goodbye, Stephen," she said. She dropped her keys on the table and walked out.

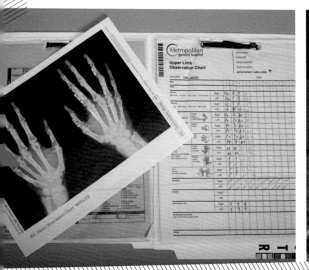

Jonathan Pangborn was playing a ball game when Strange finally found him. Strange called to him.

A tall man with dark hair and a short beard turned around.

Strange told him his name. "I'm a surgeon—*was* a surgeon," he said.

"Ah, yes," Pangborn replied coldly. "I spoke to your secretary once. You refused to see me. I wasn't *interesting*."

"You broke your back. There wasn't anything that I could do. But now you can walk again. That's not possible. How did you do it? I ..."

Strange held up his shaking hands. The damage was clear.

Pangborn looked at Strange and his hands. He thought for a minute.

"All right," he said. And he explained. When his body was broken, nobody could help. So, he decided to work with his mind. He visited teachers in far parts of the world.

"And at last I found my teacher," he said quietly. "And ..."

Strange finished his sentence: "... now you can walk again."

"Yes," Pangborn said. "There were more secrets to learn. But I came back home."

He looked away for a second, and then said quietly, "You're looking for a place called Kamar-Taj. But the cost is high."

"How much?"

"I'm not talking about *money*," Pangborn said. "Good luck."

And he went back to the game.

"This isn't the end. You can find meaning in other things."

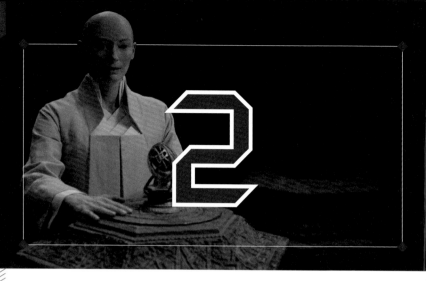

Strange Meets the Ancient One

Strange found books that described Kamar-Taj. It was in Kathmandu, the capital of Nepal. A week later, Strange was there, looking for Kamar-Taj. He walked around the city for many days, asking people about it. But nobody knew the place. Then, one day, he was going down a quiet street when two men walked toward him. He turned around and saw another man. Strange knew what the men wanted.

"Guys, I don't have any money," he said.

"Your watch," one of the men said in English.

"No, please, my watch is all that I have!" Strange said.

"Your watch!" the man repeated.

"All right," Strange said.

He felt very angry and hit the man in the face—it really hurt his hand. One of the other men hit him, and he fell to the ground. The men kicked him again and again. Someone pulled the watch off his wrist.

Suddenly, another man appeared. His face was covered, and he wore a green and black cloak. He quickly knocked all three men to the ground. They got up and ran away. Strange stood up. His body ached, and his arm really hurt.

The man picked up Strange's watch and gave it to him.

"You're looking for Kamar-Taj," he said.

How does he know? Strange thought.

"Yes," he replied.

The man started walking, and Strange followed him through the streets. They came to a wooden door.

"Are you sure this is the right place?" Strange asked.

The man looked into Strange's eyes. "Can I make a suggestion? Forget everything you know," he said.

"Uh … all right."

This is stupid, Strange thought. *But I need help.*

They went inside the building, and the man said, "This is the home of our teacher, the Ancient One."

"The Ancient One?" Strange said. "What's his real name?"

The man looked at him without speaking.

They walked into a large room with big windows. An older man was reading. Two women took Strange's coat. Then, a woman in a white robe brought him tea.

"Thank you," Strange said. He turned to the older man. "Thank you, Ancient One … for seeing me."

"You're very welcome," said the woman in white.

"Can I make a suggestion? Forget everything you know," he said.

Her head was shaved. It was difficult to guess her age. Strange looked at her, surprised.

"The Ancient One," said the man in the green and black cloak.

"Thank you, Master Mordo," the Ancient One said to the man. Then, she said, "Mr. Strange."

"Doctor," he said, drinking his tea.

"Not now," she said, smiling. "Isn't that why you're here? You've had seven operations, is that right?"

How does she know that? Strange thought.

"Yes," he replied.

She went to a low table and began making more tea.

"Did you help a man called Pangborn?" he asked. "He couldn't walk. You helped him to walk again."

"Yes," she said, smiling.

"How did you do it?" he asked.

"He couldn't walk. But *I* knew that he could walk again. And he believed me. Your body can repair itself in many different ways."

Strange felt very excited. "You can teach the body to repair itself?"

"No, Mr. Strange, I can teach a person's *spirit* to repair the body."

Strange didn't believe this. But Pangborn could walk and play ball games.

"All ... all right. How do we do that?" he asked.

The Ancient One showed Strange a book with a picture of the body. The picture showed special energy points in the body. Most scientists didn't believe in these energy points.

"Oh!" he said. "I've seen that picture before. In gift stores."

The Ancient One laughed. Strange couldn't believe it. This was stupid.

Maybe they only wanted money. He was very tired. His hand hurt. He started to shout. "I used my last dollar to get here. And you say that my spirit can repair my body. Really?"

The Ancient One answered calmly. "You've tried hard to understand the world. But you only see a *part* of the world, not the complete picture."

"I don't believe in magical energy. I don't believe in the power of belief. And a person *doesn't* have a spirit," Strange replied angrily.

"You don't understand yourself," the Ancient One said, smiling.

"Oh, *you* think you understand me. You don't. But *I* understand *you!*"

Strange pointed angrily at her. Moving very fast, the Ancient One took his arm. She pushed hard on his chest, and something very strange happened. For a few seconds, he was outside himself, looking at his own body from across the room. Then, the Ancient One waved her arms, and he was inside his body again.

"What did you just do to me?" he asked.

"I pushed your astral body out of your body," she said.

Strange believed her. "What just happened?" he asked.

"You traveled into the Astral Dimension. In the Astral Dimension, the spirit exists away from the body."

"Why are you doing this to me?" Strange asked.

Calmly, she said, "There is so much that you don't know. I want to show you *how* much. Open your eyes!"

Everything around Strange changed. He flew up and out of Kamar-Taj, and into the sky, above the clouds. He felt very scared and screamed. He could see the Earth and blue sky against the blackness of space. Then, he fell down a hole in space. Colors and energy were spinning around

Calmly, she said, "There is so much that you don't know. I want to show you *how* much. Open your eyes!"

him, and he fell through strange shapes. What were they? Were they worlds? He didn't know.

"You think you understand this world," said the voice of the Ancient One.

His body became many bodies, then came back together again. He fell down a shining yellow hole.

"What is real?" her voice continued. "Only the universe that you know?"

Hundreds of hands appeared. Then, everything changed again. He fell through a very large eye into space again.

"This universe doesn't end. There are worlds and worlds and worlds. Some are good, some are full of hate. There are dark places, and powers that are older than time."

He saw another eye, full of power and hate. Strange screamed when it saw him ... Then, it was gone. Now, there were colored lights all around him. He moved through space again, faster and faster.

"Who are you in this Multiverse, Mr. Strange?" the Ancient One asked.

He crashed back into the world, falling through the roof of Kamar-Taj onto the floor.

"Have you seen that before in a gift store?" the Ancient One asked softly.

Slowly, Strange got onto his knees, and held out his shaking hands. Now, he believed. Mordo was right. *I must forget everything I know,* he thought.

"Teach me," he said.

The Ancient One looked at him. "No," she said softly.

Mordo threw Strange out onto the street. The door closed.

"No!" Strange shouted. "No, no, no, no!"

He ran to the door and knocked hard on it. It hurt his hands.

"Open the door! Please!" he shouted.

But nobody answered.

Five hours later, Strange was still knocking on the door. Finally, he sat down with his back against it. The door opened, and Mordo pulled him inside.

"Thank you," Strange said gratefully. Without speaking, Mordo took him to a small, plain room.

"Sleep!" Mordo said.

He left, and Strange took his watch out of his pocket. The glass front was broken. He looked at the back of the watch. It had these words on it: *Time will tell how much I love you—Christine.*

"The language of the mystic arts is very old," the Ancient One said. "Sorcerers called this language 'spells.'"

She and Strange were on their knees. Waving her arms, the Ancient One drew a line of bright orange energy in the air. She turned the line, and it became a circle. A square appeared around the circle, and then smaller circles appeared.

"We use energy that comes from other dimensions of the Multiverse," she said. "We use this energy to cast spells. We also use it to make weapons."

The center circle began to turn, like a magical machine. Strange watched, surprised.

"How can I ever learn to do that?" he asked.

"How did you learn to become a surgeon?"

"Many years of study and practice," he replied.

She looked at him, and he understood. *Study and practice,* he thought. *I can do that.*

The Ancient One told Strange to read some of the books in Kamar-Taj's large library. He read them fast, and then read other books, and then more books. When he went to the library for the second time, he met the librarian.

"Hello," Strange said.

"Mr. Strange," said the librarian.

Everyone knows me here, Strange thought.

"Uh ... call me Stephen, please. And you are?"

"Wong."

"Wong," Strange repeated. "Just Wong? Like Adele?"

It was a joke, but Wong didn't smile. He pointed to the books that Strange had in his arms.

"Did you finish all these books?" he asked.

"Yes," Strange said.

He was a fast reader, and a fast learner.

"Come with me," Wong said.

Strange followed him to another part of the library.

"This part is for Masters only. But if I agree, other sorcerers can use it." He pulled two books from the shelves. "You should start with these."

Strange saw a line of books high on the wall. "What are those?" he asked.

"The Ancient One's books. Only she can do the spells in them. They're too difficult for other sorcerers."

Strange went to the books, and opened one. He couldn't read the language. But he could see that some pages were not there.

"That's *The Book of Cagliostro*. It's a book about time," Wong told him. "One of the spells in the book was stolen by a Master called Kaecilius. Before he stole the book, he killed the librarian. He cut off his head."

Wong took two more books from another shelf and turned to Strange. "I look after these books. If a book is stolen again, I'll know. And you'll be dead before you leave here."

He gave the books to Strange.

"All right," Strange said. He picked up the books. "I've enjoyed talking to you. Thank you for the books and the scary story!"

One morning, the students at Kamar-Taj were practicing their magical exercises while Mordo and Wong watched. The other students could make shining lines of energy. Strange could do the movements, but he couldn't make the energy lines. He didn't ask for help, and nobody offered to help him.

Mordo gave the students sling rings, and they put them over two fingers.

"You need to be able to use these," he said. "With sling rings, we can travel through the Multiverse. To travel to a place, you must first see it in your mind. Imagine it clearly."

The students began to make portals, but Strange couldn't do this.

"And stop," said Mordo, when the Ancient One appeared.

"I'd like to talk to Mr. Strange alone," she said.

Everyone left.

"My hands," Strange said. *That's the problem,* he thought.

"Magic is not about your hands," the Ancient One said. "You cannot give orders to a river. You have to move *with* the river. Your intelligence has taken you a long way in life, Stephen. But it won't help you now. You need to forget about yourself. When you do that, your power will grow." She drew a portal in the air. "Come with me."

Surprised, Strange followed the Ancient One through the portal. They came out onto a mountainside. There was a very strong wind, and it was snowing. It was also freezing.

"You have about two minutes before your body shuts down," she said.

"What?"

"Forget about yourself, Stephen," the Ancient One said, almost singing

Surprised, Strange followed the Ancient One through the portal. They came out onto a mountainside.

the words. She passed through the portal to Kamar-Taj again, and closed it behind her.

"No, no! Don't!" Strange cried.

He tried to get through the portal, but fell on the snow.

In Kamar-Taj, Mordo asked the Ancient One, "How is he?"

"We shall see," she said. Her hands were moving nervously.

"Maybe I should ..." Mordo suggested.

She stopped him. They waited ... and waited ...

A portal appeared, and Strange fell through it onto the ground. There was ice in his beard and mustache. He lifted himself up to look at the Ancient One. Then, he fell to the ground again.

Alone in his room, Strange thought about his time on the mountainside. He was so scared. But he could make magic! Now, he knew that it was real. There was a new, dark red robe in his room. He wasn't a student now.

I've changed. I need to look different, he thought. Slowly, he cut his hair, and shaved off most of his beard and mustache. His hands still shook, but he could do these things now. He looked at himself in the mirror. He was a new man.

Slowly, he cut his hair, and shaved off most of his beard and mustache.

Strange Finds the Eye of Agamotto

When Strange went into the library again, Wong saw something different about him.

"What do you want?" the librarian asked.

"Books on astral projection."

"You're not ready for that."

"Oh, give me the books!"

"No."

Strange decided to take the books. He practiced making portals, again and again. *If I can make a portal, I can get through one, into the library*, he thought. Soon, he could make portals easily. He stole the books that he needed from the library. He worked very hard and learned a lot. But there was so much more to learn.

The Ancient One asked him to see her.

"Your teachers tell me that you question them in every lesson. You like to teach yourself," she said.

"I can't accept rules that seem stupid," Strange replied.

"Students mustn't make portals into the library. That's a rule."

Oh, Strange thought. *Wong knows that I've done that.*

"Did Wong tell you?" he asked.

"You're learning very fast," the sorcerer replied. "You need a safe space to practice your spells."

She waved her arm, and a wall appeared in the middle of the room. It was like a mirror broken into a thousand pieces. She walked toward this wall and passed through it. Strange followed her.

"You're now inside the Mirror Dimension," the Ancient One said. "The other students and sorcerers in this room can't see it. Things happen in here, but they don't change the real world. We use the Mirror Dimension to practice magic. There are things that are very dangerous for our world. Sometimes we can put them here. And then the world is safe."

There's so much that I don't know, Strange thought. *I must work harder.*

Later, outside, Mordo taught Strange martial arts exercises. It was important for a sorcerer to learn martial arts.

"How old is the Ancient One?" Strange asked Mordo.

"Nobody knows—she never talks about her past."

"You don't know about her past, but you follow her," Strange said. He didn't understand this.

"If she says something, you can believe it. I've learned that," Mordo replied. "And she's kind. She made me the person that I am today."

The two men prepared to fight.

"Believe in your teacher," Mordo said. "And don't leave the path."

"Like Kaecilius?" Strange asked.

"That's right," Mordo said.

He spun Strange around, and pressed Strange tightly against his chest. Strange couldn't get free. Mordo spoke in Strange's ear.

"When Kaecilius came to us, he was an unhappy man. He was looking for answers in the mystic arts. He was an excellent student, but proud. He questioned the Ancient One's teaching."

Ah, Strange thought. *I question the Ancient One's teaching. Mordo thinks that I'm following the same path as Kaecilius. He's going to be surprised.*

He hit Mordo hard in the stomach and got free.

Mordo stood up, smiling. "Kaecilius left Kamar-Taj," he told Strange. "Some students went with him."

"He stole those pages with the spell about time, didn't he?" Strange asked.

"Yes."

"What did the spell do?"

"No more questions," Mordo said.

He went to the wall, and picked up a short, wooden stick.

"What's that?" Strange asked.

"Some magic is very powerful. Sorcerers can only hold it for a short time," Mordo explained. "So we put this magic into *things.* We call these things 'relics.' This is one of them."

He held the stick with both hands, and it became bright with magical energy.

"There are many relics," he continued. "For example, the Vaulting Boots of Valtorr."

As Mordo spoke, he kicked his feet together. He was wearing boots, and light came from them.

"When do I get a relic?" Strange asked.

"When you're ready."

"I think I'm ready."

"The relic decides when you're ready," Mordo said, smiling. "But now, make a weapon."

Holding his hands in front of him, Strange produced a line of energy. Mordo suddenly hit it with the relic.

"Fight!" Mordo shouted. "Fight! Imagine that I want to kill you!"

He jumped very high over Strange, using the Vaulting Boots. Then he kicked Strange in the chest, and Strange fell to the ground.

"Maybe one day, someone *will* try to kill you!" Mordo shouted.

Strange often thought about Christine. He wanted to see her. *I write to her but she never replies,* he thought. *What can I say?* Then he had an idea. *When I see Christine, I'll say sorry,* he thought. *I hurt her badly.*

Strange was learning to be less proud. He started thinking about all his mistakes in the past. *The Book of Cagliostro* was about the study of time. *Can I change the past? Is it possible?* he asked himself.

Late that night, he went to the library, and took *The Book of Cagliostro* from its place on the shelf. He could understand the language now. He began to read, eating an apple at the same time. There was a symbol on one of the pages. Strange looked at the symbol carefully. It was called "The Eye of Agamotto." Strange looked up. The Eye was there in the library, only three meters away from him.

"Wong?" Strange called.

There was no answer. He was alone. He picked up the Eye of Agamotto, and hung it around his neck. Then, he returned to the book.

"O.K." he said quietly, reading from the book. "First, open the Eye of Agamotto."

He touched the middle and fourth fingers of both hands together. The Eye of Agamotto opened, shining with a green light.

He put his hands together and turned them in a circle. A circle of green light with smaller squares and circles in the center appeared between his hands. The circle was as big as his hand. Two small, green circles appeared around his right arm.

Strange pointed the large, green circle at the apple that he was eating.

He put his hands together and turned them in a circle.

Then he turned the circle to the right. More of the apple disappeared. *This is the future!* Strange thought. He turned the circle to the left, and the apple became complete again.

"Oh!" Strange said excitedly. He was able to change time. He looked at the book again. *Kaecilius pulled out pages that described a powerful spell,* he remembered.

He found the place in the book. Slowly, he turned the green circle to the left, pointing it at the book. The pages appeared. Nobody in Kamar-Taj wanted to talk about the spell. Now, at last, Strange could learn about it.

He studied the page on the right. There was a large, red symbol on it. The other page described a spell.

"'Dormammu,'" Strange read. "'The Dark Dimension. Life without end.'"

How is the Ancient One so old? Strange asked himself. *Maybe she's using the energy of the Dark Dimension. Can this be true? How does she do it?*

Strange believed that the Ancient One was good. She wanted to do good in the world. But this was very dangerous.

He could feel new power in himself. He began to turn the green circle. A portal appeared in the air over the table. It looked like glass—it was like the Mirror Dimension portal, but bigger. The energy was stronger. In his mind, Strange saw the portal opening. The portal began to open.

"Stop!" Mordo shouted angrily. The portal and the green circle disappeared. "You must not change time!"

"I ... I was only doing the spell in the book," Strange said.

Wong was there, too.

"And what did the book say about the dangers?" he asked.

"I haven't read that part yet," Strange said.

He started to understand. *Maybe I needed to be more careful*, he thought.

"You were changing time!" Mordo shouted. "It's very dangerous. You can make time loops by mistake. If you do that, the same things will happen again and again. The loop won't stop—and you will be in it!"

"You're lucky that you didn't die," Wong said angrily. He closed *The Book of Cuyliostro*, and put it back in its place. "We do not *change* the natural law. We *defend* it," he said.

Mordo was looking at Strange in a new way.

"How did you learn to follow all the spells and open the portal?" he asked.

"I have a very good memory," Strange said.

"You were also born for the mystic arts," Mordo said.

"But my hands still shake," said Strange.

"Maybe that will change," Wong said.

Oh, good! Strange thought. "Who are we? Tell me! What do we *do* here?" he asked.

Wong looked at Mordo. Then he said, "Sorcerers protect the world from mystical dangers. There have been Ancient Ones for thousands of years. Agamotto was the father of the mystic arts. He was the sorcerer who made the Eye. He built Sanctums in places of power."

Wong pointed to three doors in the wall behind the Eye.

"That is the door to the Hong Kong Sanctum, and that door is to the New York Sanctum. That one, to the London Sanctum. There are lines of energy between them."

"The Sanctums protect the world, and we sorcerers protect the Sanctums. Each Sanctum has a Master," Mordo explained.

"Why do the Sanctums need protection?" asked Strange.

"There are living things in other dimensions that want to attack our universe," Wong replied.

"Like Dormammu?"

"Where did you learn that name?" Mordo asked.

"I just read it in *The Book of Cagliostro*. Why?"

"Dormammu lives in the Dark Dimension. Time does not exist there. He destroys worlds. He has great power. He wants to bring all worlds into his Dark Dimension. He wants our world most of all."

Strange was beginning to understand. "The pages that Kaecilius stole ..."

"They are a spell to find Dormammu. Kaecilius wants to take power from the Dark Dimension."

"Uhh ... O.K." Strange laughed. It sounded crazy. "O.K. I ... I came here because of my hands. I'm a doctor. Are you fighting a mystical war? I don't want to do that."

There was a sudden sound. Wong looked at one of the doors.

"London," he said. The London portal opened. A man ran into the room and fell dead on the floor.

Strange Fights Kaecilius and His Zealots

Through the open portal, Strange saw a tall man wearing a sorcerer's robe. The skin around his eyes was gray and purple and looked very strange. His eyes burned with power and hate.

"Kaecilius!" Wong shouted. "No!"

Kaecilius lifted his arms and brought them down. A large ball of golden energy appeared.

There was a sudden, loud *BANG!* Parts of the wall fell down, and small fires started burning. Strange was blown through another door and fell to the floor. He got up. He tried to go back through the door, but it was closed. *Where am I?* he thought.

"Wong?" he called. "Mordo?"

There was no answer. Strange walked into a very large room. He could see the entrance to the building, and walked outside. Turning around, he noticed the building's address: 177A Bleecker Street. He was in New York City, in Greenwich Village. He stepped back and looked up. High on the building was the sign of the New York Sanctum.

Where's the Master? Strange thought. *I must find him!* The Zealots were attacking London, and Kamar-Taj was damaged, too.

He went back into the Sanctum.

"Hello?" he called, but there was no answer.

He went upstairs. There, he found a room with three large glass doors. There was something different behind each door. From left to right, there was a forest, the ocean, and a mountain. There was a large, metal wheel next to the doors. Strange turned it, and the ocean in the center door changed to sand.

Another large room was full of glass cases with different things inside them. There was a red cloak in one of them. It moved as he walked toward it.

Then, Strange heard sounds from downstairs. He went to the top of the stairs and looked down. There was a man standing opposite the front door. Kaecilius and two Zealots, a man and a woman, came in through the door.

"Daniel, I see that you're Master of this Sanctum," Kaecilius said to the man.

So that's Daniel Drumm, Strange thought. The Masters at Kamar-Taj sometimes talked about him.

"Do you know what that means?" Drumm replied.

"It means that you'll protect the Sanctum. And you are ready to die for it."

Kaecilius made a Space Shard between his hands. The two men began fighting, and the Zealots attacked Drumm, too. He fought well, but Kaecilius was using the power of Dormammu. He was much more powerful. Strange shouted as Kaecilius pushed his Space Shard deep into Drumm's stomach.

Kaecilius looked up. He pulled the Space Shard out of Drumm's stomach, and Drumm fell to the floor.

"How long have you been at Kamar-Taj, Mr. ...?" Kaecilius asked.

"*Doctor,*" Strange corrected him.

Kaecilius looked surprised.

"Mr. Doctor?"

"It's Strange."

"Maybe," said Kaecilius. He didn't understand.

Kaecilius pushed the Space Shard into Drumm again. Seeing this,

Strange quickly made an energy whip. Kaecilius ran up the wall to the next floor, and he and Strange started fighting. The Zealots attacked, too. Strange ran farther into the Sanctum, toward the glass doors. He couldn't fight Kaecilius and both Zealots alone. Behind him, Kaecilius cast a spell. The glass doors started moving farther away as Kaecilius came closer. He walked across the top of the room toward Strange. Then he folded the room around him, spinning it.

Strange was thrown all around the place. He hung onto something that was high on a wall. Below him, one of the Zealots stood in front of the center glass door. It was the one with sand behind it. Strange had an idea. He fell all the way down, hitting the Zealot with both feet. He pushed her through the door. Then, he stood up, and turned the metal wheel. The sand disappeared, and now there were tall trees. The Zealot couldn't return. The other Zealot attacked him and he did the same thing. The Zealots were gone. But there was still Kaecilius.

Kaecilius made another pair of Space Shards. Strange ran into the room with the glass cases. Kaecilius followed, and kicked him into a glass case. Strange got up. The sorcerer kicked him into another glass case, the one with the red cloak.

He's going to kill me, Strange thought.

Kaecilius hit him again and again, then kicked him down toward the floor below.

But as Strange was falling, the red cloak dropped over his shoulders. He stopped falling. A few seconds later, Kaecilius saw Doctor Strange in the air above the stairs. The Eye of Agamotto shone on Strange's chest.

Strange felt a new power moving in him. He remembered Mordo's words: "The relic decides when you're ready." This was exactly the right time!

He made another energy whip, and hit Kaecilius's Space Shard with it. Kaecilius pulled his weapon toward him, and Strange fell to the floor. He got up, and the cloak pulled him away from Kaecilius. What was it doing? Kaecilius came toward him. Then Strange understood. The cloak was telling him something. On the wall behind him was a jacket made of pieces of metal. Strange pulled it from the wall and threw it at Kaecilius.

It fell over the sorcerer's body, and he couldn't move. Even his mouth was covered.

Kaecilius tried to say something. Strange uncovered his mouth.

"You'll die here," the sorcerer said calmly.

"Oh, stop it," Strange said.

"You cannot stop this, Mr. Doctor. It's the end and the beginning," Kaecilius said softly.

"My name is Doctor Strange."

"You *are* a doctor." Kaecilius sounded surprised.

"Yes."

"A scientist. So, you understand. All things get older. All things die. But the Dark Dimension is a place that has no time. The world doesn't have to die, Doctor. This world can become part of the One. The great and beautiful One. And death will not exist. People think of good and bad. But time is the real problem. Time kills everything. People want a world without time. Death is terrible. Doctor ... we want to save the world. We want to give it to Dormammu. He is the reason for everything that exists."

"The Ancient One *protects* life," Strange said.

Kaecilius didn't reply, but asked, "Why did you go to Kamar-Taj, Doctor? Did you want power? You went because you needed help. Everyone in Kamar-Taj was damaged in some way. The Ancient One helped us and taught us spells. But she keeps the real magic for herself. How has she lived so long? Have you ever asked yourself that?"

"I ... I saw the spell in *The Book of Cagliostro*."

"So, you know." Kaecilius sounded pleased. "The spell gives me the power to win against the Ancient One. I can destroy the Sanctums, and the Dark Dimension can come into this world. Dormammu doesn't destroy worlds—he *saves* worlds."

"But Dormammu made you a murderer," Strange replied.

Kaecilius smiled. "You've lost your sling ring, Doctor."

Strange looked down. It was true. His sling ring was gone. He turned around, and a Space Shard flew deep into his chest. A Zealot was running up the stairs toward him. He threw Strange down the stairs. Strange knew that he was very badly hurt. The Zealot followed him down the stairs, and made another Space Shard.

But then the red cloak pulled away from Strange's body. It fell on the Zealot's head and pulled him to the ground. Strange's sling ring appeared from inside the cloak. The cloak threw the ring across the floor toward him. Strange put it on, then stood up. He knew where to go. He tried to make a portal. He had almost no energy, and it was very difficult. But the portal appeared. On the other side, he could see a hospital closet. Slowly, he walked through the portal into the closet. Behind him, the Zealot was still fighting with the cloak.

Strange almost fell out of the closet into the hospital. A nurse ran toward him.

It fell over the sorcerer's body, and he couldn't move.

"Sir, can I help you?" she said.

"Dr. Palmer, where is she?" Strange said, speaking with difficulty.

"Sir, we need to ..."

"Where is she?" Strange shouted.

"At the nurses' desk."

Strange found her. Every minute was important.

"Christine!"

She ran to him.

"Stephen! Oh, no! What ...?"

"I need an operation, *now,*" he said. "Only you. Now! I don't have any time!"

She took him to an operating room and put him on a table. "What happened?"

"A knife in the chest."

She started working.

"What are you wearing?" she asked.

Strange didn't reply. He knew there was blood around his heart. He told Christine this, and she prepared to take it away. But he was getting weaker and weaker. His arms dropped to his sides. *I'm going to die,* he thought.

"No, no, no, no, no, no! Stephen! Stephen!" Christine cried.

I need to show Christine the exact position of the blood, Strange thought. *If she does this wrong, I'll die.*

Then, he had an idea. Astral projection. He pulled his astral body up and out of his body. Now, his astral body was above the operating table. He looked down and saw his real body there.

"Please be careful," he said.

Christine screamed, and jumped away.

"Stephen? What am I seeing?"

"My astral body."

"Are you dead?"

"No, Christine, but I *am* dying."

"O.K. O.K."

Strange used his astral fingers to show her the exact place in his chest. He watched her work. The skin above his heart was the color of the skin

Now, his astral body was above the operating table.

around Kaecilius's eyes.

"I've never seen anything like this before," she said. "What did this to you?"

"I don't know," Strange said.

Then, the astral body of one of the Zealots came into the room.

"I'm going to disappear now," Strange's astral body told Christine.

"No, I ..."

"Keep me alive, please!"

Strange disappeared and turned toward the Zealot. They started fighting. The Zealot was much better at martial arts than Strange. They moved through the wall into another part of the hospital. The Zealot hit Strange again and again.

Then, Strange's heart stopped. Immediately, Christine used a machine to start it again. The energy from the machine passed through Strange's astral body. It was very strong and threw the Zealot across the room.

Strange's heart started again ... but slowly. He was still in danger. His astral body appeared to Christine.

"Do it again!" he said.

She screamed, and said, "Stop doing that!"

"Do it again—but stronger this time!" Strange repeated.

"No, your heart has started."

It was dangerous to use the machine again. Strange knew that. But he needed help against the Zealot.

"Do it!"

He disappeared. The two men started fighting again. The Zealot pressed Strange close to him, and Strange didn't try to get free. Then, Christine used the machine. Its energy passed through Strange's astral body and into the Zealot. The Zealot's body shook, and he disappeared. There was a sudden, strong light, then everything went dark. On the operating table, Strange's body shook, and he opened his eyes. Christine jumped back.

"Oh! Are you O.K.?"

He tried to lift his head. "Yes," he said. He was alive.

A little later, when Christine was finishing the operation, she became very angry. "After all this time, you come here, flying out of your body," she said.

"Yes, I know," Strange said. He wanted to explain, but could she understand? "I missed you. I wrote to you, but you didn't answer," he said.

She was working on his body and didn't look at him.

"I didn't want to," she said.

"Christine, I am so, so sorry. For all of it." It felt good to say that. Strange knew that he was a different person now. "And you were right. I was unkind to you, and you were so good to me."

"Stop," she said. "This isn't the Stephen that I know."

And now, she looked at him. He saw worry—and maybe something more—in her face.

"What's happening? Where have you been?" she asked.

"After Western medicine couldn't help me, I went east to Kathmandu. I found a place called Kamar-Taj there. I talked to someone called the Ancient One, and ..."

"So you joined a strange religious group."

"No, I didn't. Not exactly. I mean, they taught me to use special powers. I didn't know these powers existed."

"It seems a *very* strange group."

Strange laughed, and sat up. "I'm late for a meeting," he said.

Christine helped him to walk out of the operating room. "This is crazy," she said.

"Yes," Strange agreed.

"Where are you going?"

"Um ..." He wasn't sure how to say it.

"Really," Christine said. "Tell me the *true* story."

O.K, I will, thought Strange. "There's a powerful sorcerer who can change the natural laws. He tried very hard to kill me. But I left him in Greenwich Village, and I'm going back there through a portal in a closet."

Christine moved away. "O.K. *Don't* tell me," she said. "That's fine."

Strange opened the closet door. The portal was still there, and he could see the New York Sanctum inside it. Christine walked toward it to check. It was real! Her eyes were wide with surprise.

Strange walked through the portal. He turned back to her.

"I have to go," he said.

The portal closed.

Kaecilius Fights the Ancient One

The Zealot's body was in the Sanctum hall, and the cloak was near it. Strange put two fingers on the man's neck. He was dead. *I killed him,* Strange thought. He felt terrible. But he had no time to think about it. He put the cloak around his shoulders and went upstairs. Kaecilius wasn't there.

"Strange!"

He turned and saw Mordo.

"You're O.K." Mordo said.

"Yes, I'm O.K."

"The Cloak of Levitation," Mordo said. "It came to you."

"You did well." The Ancient One stepped out of the shadows.

"Kaecilius has escaped," Strange replied. "He can fold space and things in the real world, outside the Mirror Dimension."

The Ancient One looked very worried. "He's destroyed the London Sanctum," she said. "Only New York and Hong Kong can protect us from the Dark Dimension now. You saved the New York Sanctum. But its Master is dead. It needs another one ... *Master* Strange."

Master? That's not possible, Strange thought. *I'm not ready.*

"No," he said, turning to her. "It is *Dr.* Strange. Not Strange, not Mr. Strange—*Dr.* Strange." He felt terrible. "I'm a doctor and I've just killed a man! I'm not going to do that again! I became a doctor to save lives. I don't want to kill people."

"You became a doctor to save *your* life," the Ancient One replied. "You are interested in yourself most of all. You think you can change things— even death. But nobody can do that."

"And Dormammu? He promises that with him, we won't die."

"Our fear of death is food for Dormammu," the Ancient One said.

"You talk to me about death," said Strange. "But I know how you've lived so long. I saw the spells in *The Book of Cagliostro.*"

"Be very careful about your next words, Doctor," she said. Her voice was quiet and hard.

"Because maybe you won't like them?" Strange asked.

"Maybe you don't understand."

"What is he talking about?" asked Mordo, looking at the Ancient One.

"We're talking about her long life. She takes power from the Dark Dimension to stay alive," Strange replied.

"That's not true," Mordo said. He looked at the Ancient One again, waiting for her reply. But she was looking at Strange, and her face didn't change.

"I've seen the spells," Strange said.

"The Zealots will return," the Ancient One said. "You'll need help."

She turned and left. There was a short silence.

"You don't know her, Mordo," Strange said finally.

"You can't say that," Mordo said angrily. "You don't understand the importance of her work."

"No, and I don't *want* to understand."

"You're scared," Mordo said. He was starting to get angry.

"Because I'm not a killer?"

"These Zealots will kill us, but you don't want to kill them first."

"I just killed a Zealot," Strange shouted.

"You did that to save yourself!" Mordo shouted. "And then you felt bad about it."

"Is it easy for you to kill?"

"You don't know the things that I've done ... The answer is yes, when it's necessary."

The two men were standing very close, both very angry now.

"You're not a brave man, Stephen," Mordo said.

There was the sound of a portal opening.

"They've returned," Mordo said.

They ran to look down into the hall. Kaecilius and two Zealots were there. There was a large, shining ball of magical power in front of Kaecilius.

"We have to end this. Now!" Mordo said angrily.

He jumped down to the floor below. Strange jumped, too, but the Cloak of Levitation held him in the air. Mordo started fighting with both Zealots. Kaecilius began casting a spell.

That spell will destroy the New York Sanctum, Strange thought.

The Zealots were holding Mordo tightly.

"Strange!" Mordo cried. "Get down here and fight!"

But Strange had a plan. He opened his arms, and cast a spell. Kaecilius brought both arms down. There was a loud noise. Strange was hanging in the air above the stairs. Kaecilius looked up, surprised.

"The Mirror Dimension," Strange said. "You can't change the real world in here."

Kaecilius smiled and moved his hands. The stairs below Strange broke into two pieces. Things began to move around them. It was very dangerous. Strange flew down the stairs. He pulled the sling ring from Kaecilius's finger, and ran out of the door. Mordo freed himself from the Zealots and ran with him.

"I've got Kaecilius's sling ring," Strange told Mordo. "They can't escape, can they?"

They turned around to look. Kaecilius and his Zealots came out.

"Run!" cried Mordo.

They ran down Bleecker Street to Sixth Avenue. When they got there, the buildings and streets started moving around them.

"Because they get power from the Dark Dimension, they're more powerful in the Mirror Dimension," Mordo said. "This isn't the real world, but they can kill us here. That wasn't smart, Strange!"

Kaecilius and the two Zealots were running toward them, and Strange and Mordo started running again. Buildings and streets were breaking into pieces. Strange opened a portal in front of them. He planned to escape, and leave Kaecilius in the Mirror Dimension. Then, buildings started falling on their sides. Strange and Mordo were thrown across the street, and hit the side of a bus.

They got up and jumped up the side of a tall building. Strange wore the Cloak of Levitation, and Mordo wore the Vaulting Boots of Valtorr. Kaecilius and his Zealots followed them. Strange opened another portal in front of them. Then, Kaecilius jumped in the air. When he came down, a wave of energy moved up the building. The portal disappeared. Kaecilius waved his hands. The building broke into two pieces, and the two men fell off it into the air.

All around them, buildings started falling. The two men fell onto the side of one of them. It moved, and they both fell a long way down. Strange fell onto some steps. Things were moving all the time, and he was high above the city.

Then, Kaecilius saw him. He ran toward Strange and hit him hard. Strange fell, and Kaecilius took back his sling ring. Then he made a Space Shard. Strange was down on the ground and couldn't move.

Suddenly, the ground under Strange pulled away from Kaecilius, and there was the Ancient One. She was wearing the yellow robe that she wore for fighting. Opening her arms, she made bright half-circles of energy.

They got up and jumped up the side of a tall building.

Strange stood up, and Mordo came and stood next to him. He was looking at the Ancient One. On her face was the symbol of Dormammu. Kaecilius and the Zealots had the same symbol on their faces.

"It's true," said Mordo, sounding surprised and hurt. "She takes power from the Dark Dimension."

The Ancient One looked at him. Her face showed nothing. Then, she turned to look at Kaecilius.

Pieces of the city were moving around them. This was their final meeting.

"When I came to you, I was very unhappy," Kaecilius said. "You were my teacher, and I believed in you. But you lied to me."

"I tried to protect you," The Ancient One replied.

"From what?"

"From yourself."

"I have a new teacher now."

"Dormammu is lying to you. You know nothing about him," she said sadly. The symbol of Dormammu was gone from her face now. "Life with Dormammu is terrible."

"That's not true!" Kaecilius said angrily.

The two Zealots were at his side. They walked toward the Ancient One and attacked her. Moving with great speed and power, she pushed them away from her. They returned, and she knocked one to the ground. She pressed the other one against her and held an energy circle against his neck. She chose not to kill him.

Kaecilius came close, and pushed his Space Shard through the Zealot's body and into the Ancient One. Mordo shouted in fear. Kaecilius pulled out the Space Shard, and the Zealot fell to the floor. Kaecilius kicked the Ancient One hard, and she flew through the air. There was a portal there, and her body passed through it.

Strange and Mordo ran through the portal just before it closed. The Ancient One fell down and down, until she crashed through glass onto the sidewalk of a busy street. People screamed. Many ran to look. Strange and Mordo reached the ground a few seconds later.

Strange felt the Ancient One's body. Her head was badly hurt.

I know where to go, he thought.

Death of the Ancient One

A few minutes later, Strange was in a hospital room with the Ancient One.

"Christine!" Strange shouted.

Christine heard Strange's voice and closed her eyes.

"Again?" she said. "Are you joking?" Then she saw the Ancient One. "Oh!" she cried, and ran toward Strange.

"The patient's heart has stopped," Strange said, and explained the problems.

They took the Ancient One to an operating room, and Strange prepared to operate. But when he lifted his hands, they shook. *I can't do this*, he thought.

There was another surgeon there who was good at his work. Strange asked him to do the operation. The surgeon started to prepare.

Then, Christine cried, "We're losing her!"

The Ancient One was dying.

Strange took his astral body out of his body. The astral body of the Ancient One was moving slowly out of the room.

"What are you doing? You're dying!" Strange cried to her.

She didn't answer. He followed her through the hospital, and she stopped at a wall of windows. There, she looked out at the city.

"You have to return to your body now," Strange said urgently. "You don't have time."

But then, he looked out the window. Nothing was moving. *Time has stopped, or almost stopped,* he thought. It was dark, but there was a strange light in the sky.

"I've looked into the future at this point in time for many years. But I can't see past it," the Ancient One said.

"You think that you'll die here," Strange said.

She didn't reply to this, but said, "I never saw *your* future. But I know what is possible for you. You have so much goodness in you. You were always very successful. But it wasn't because you wanted success. It was because you were afraid of failing."

"That made me a great doctor."

"No, it did the opposite. You were too proud and too afraid. You didn't learn the most important lesson of all."

"What's that?"

The Ancient One turned to look at him. "It's not about you," she said, with great love.

She waited for him to speak, but he said nothing. It was better to listen. He knew that now.

"When you came to me, you asked about Pangborn," she said. "*I* didn't help him. Pangborn takes energy from the Dark Dimension into his body."

"He uses magic to walk," Strange said.

"All the time. He had to choose. He could return to his life in New York, or work for something bigger than himself."

"You mean, my hands can get better. And I can be a surgeon again?"

"That's possible. But the world needs you."

So, that's it, Strange thought. *I can be a surgeon again, or I can protect the world from Dormammu.*

"I've hated taking power from the Dark Dimension," the Ancient One continued. "But I had to do it to protect the world. Sometimes, we must go against the natural laws to do something good. You know that."

"Mordo won't understand."

"Mordo is very different from you. But you work well together. He's very strong, and you are able to find different answers to a problem. You can only stop Dormammu if you work together."

Strange knew that this was true. But he was also afraid.

"I'm not ready," he said.

"People are never ready," the Ancient One said. "We don't choose our time of death."

She took his hand in hers. "Death gives meaning to life. We need to know that time is short. But after all this time, why aren't I ready?"

Now, there was even more light in the sky. Strange looked at the light, surprised. The Ancient One dropped his hand. He turned to look at her—he was alone. And the light in the sky was gone.

The Ancient One was dead. *What shall I do now?* Strange asked himself. He returned to his body. Then, he went to wash his hands. Christine came, and they washed their hands together. They often did this after operations. But everything was different now. He couldn't work as a surgeon. The Ancient One was dead. *And Christine has seen things that she can't understand*, he thought.

He took her hand in his.

"Are you O.K.?" she asked quietly, looking worried.

He didn't know. *Will I ever be O.K. again?* he thought.

He turned to look at her.

"What's happening? I don't understand," Christine said.

"I know. But I have to go away now." He held her face in his hands. "This is a new beginning for me," he said softly, looking into her eyes.

"Yes, but a very strange one," Christine said.

They both smiled. Someone was calling for Dr. Palmer.

"I don't want you to go," Strange said.

They were both almost crying. Christine kissed him softly, then turned and walked away. Strange stood there, tears falling down his face. Then, he turned. The Cloak of Levitation appeared and dropped around his shoulders. He looked at himself in the mirror. He knew what he had to do. He made a portal and stepped through it into Kamar-Taj.

7

Dormammu

Mordo stood alone in the darkness. Kamar-Taj was very badly damaged.

"She's dead," Strange said.

"You were right," Mordo said slowly. "I didn't know her."

He felt terrible about The Ancient One's death. But there was a lot that he didn't understand.

"The Dark Dimension is so dangerous," he said. "The Ancient One was wrong to use its power. Why did she do it? She took power from the Dark Dimension to get hundreds of years of life."

"She believed that it was right," Strange said. Sometimes it was right *not* to follow the rules. He knew that.

"If you do that, you pay. Don't you understand?" said Mordo. "Because of her actions, Kaecilius went to Dormammu. And this is the result."

"Mordo, the London Sanctum has fallen. And they've attacked the New York Sanctum. Twice."

It wasn't necessary to say more. They needed to act now.

"You know where they're going next," Strange said.

"Hong Kong," Mordo replied.

"I can't fight them alone."

Mordo looked at him. Strange opened a portal to Hong Kong, and they jumped through.

Everywhere, fires were burning. Water was falling through the air. Many buildings were badly damaged. People were screaming and running around wildly.

"The Sanctum's already fallen," Strange said.

The two men looked up. There were strange lights in the sky, and purple and blue clouds moved through it.

"The Dark Dimension. Dormammu is coming," Mordo said. "It's too late. Nothing can stop him."

Kaecilius was walking along the street toward them with his Zealots. He looked pleased. *It's the end of the world,* Strange thought. *But ...*

"Maybe *we* can stop them—*maybe*," he told Mordo.

He was wearing the Eye of Agamotto around his neck. He brought his fingers together, and the Eye opened.

"No," Kaecilius said, and ran toward Strange.

Strange made another movement, and brought the powerful, green circle of the Eye in front of him. Rings of power circled his arm. Kaecilius jumped through the air, holding a Space Shard. But Strange was holding the spinning green circle in front of him. Kaecilius slowed ... and then stopped. Slowly, Strange began to turn the circle toward the left.

Time began to move backward. People started moving backward. Kaecilius dropped to the ground and ran backward along the street. A sign on top of a car lifted into the air.

"The spell's successful," Mordo said.

They ran down the street toward the Sanctum, while time moved backward around them. But the Dark Dimension was close, and Kaecilius was able to use its power. He and his Zealots freed themselves from the time spell and followed them. Kaecilius kicked Strange to the ground, and the Zealots attacked Mordo. Around them, buildings were starting to repair themselves. Parts of the damaged buildings were flying up into the air.

Strange got up, but Kaecilius threw him to the ground again. Then, Strange was almost hit by a car that was going backward. He couldn't get away from Kaecilius. But Mordo got free of the Zealots and ran toward them. He used an energy whip to catch Kaecilius. He threw the sorcerer into a building.

"No!" Kaecilius shouted.

In a few seconds, the building built itself around him, and he disappeared. Near them, they saw Wong lying on the ground. He stood up, looking very surprised. Strange quickly cast a spell that put Wong outside time.

"I'm breaking the laws of the natural world, I know," Strange told him.

"Don't stop now!" Wong said.

Strange looked up. The Sanctum was slowly becoming a building again. Above it, the colors and energy of the Dark Dimension were starting to disappear.

"When the Sanctum is complete, they'll attack again. We have to defend it. Let's go!" he said.

The three men started running.

But then Kaecilius escaped from the wall that was holding him. He hit the ground with his hand. This made a wave of energy that pushed Strange, Wong, and Mordo to the ground. Time slowed … and stopped. Parts of the Sanctum hung in the air. Everyone, everywhere, stopped moving.

"Get up and fight, Strange!" Mordo cried. "We will finish this."

Mordo and Wong got up. Kaecilius and the two Zealots were walking toward them, and the two men turned to them.

"You know that I'm going to win," Kaecilius said.

His eyes were deeper in his head, and the strange, colored skin covered more of his face now. He was watching the sky.

"Isn't it beautiful? A world without time. Without death."

Strange was trying to get up. *A world without time,* he thought, and remembered reading *The Book of Cagliostro*. He also remembered Mordo's words about changing time: "It's dangerous. You can make time loops by mistake."

Kaecilius was using the power of the Dark Dimension. Strange knew that he could not win against him. But there was always more than one answer to a problem.

The Cloak of Levitation carried Strange into the air and up into the sky.

"Strange!" Mordo shouted.

Strange wanted to explain, but there wasn't time. *Soon, Kaecilius will break the time spell,* he thought. *Something must change before then … I think I know the answer.*

The sorcerers watched Strange disappearing into the Dark Dimension.

"He's gone," said Kaecilius. "Strange has chosen to go to Dormammu."

Mordo's mouth moved, but no words came out.

In the blackness of the Dark Dimension, strange, colored worlds slowly turned. Strange moved between them. They were different sizes—some very small, some very large. Some were as big as the sun. Strange saw nothing that was living. What could live there? Nothing. Only Dormammu. And Strange wanted to see him.

He came down onto a small world. There were shining, blue holes in the ground, and hot air came out of them. *I must make a time loop,* Strange thought. *Can I do it?*

He waved his hand over his left arm. Two green circles of energy started turning around his arm. The green Eye of Agamotto shone on his chest.

Near him, he saw something that looked like a blue and purple sun. Then he realized that it was one of Dormammu's eyes. Dormammu's dark body was the size of a very tall building. Strange jumped onto a larger world to get closer to him.

"Dormammu!" he shouted. "I've come to bargain."

Dormammu's face appeared over Strange. It was thirty meters high.

"You've come to die," Dormammu said. "Your world is now *my* world."

His voice sounded like rocks crashing together. He sent a powerful stream of energy toward Strange. Strange tried to fight it, screamed, … and disappeared.

"Dormammu," Strange shouted. "I've come to bargain."

"You've come to die," Dormammu said. "Your world is now *my* world. What is happening? Is this real?"

"Yes," said Strange.

"Good," Dormammu said. A few seconds later, two long, sharp stones hit Strange in the chest, and killed him.

"Dormammu," Strange shouted. "I've come to bargain."

"You ..." said Dormammu, and stopped. He didn't understand. "What is happening?" he asked.

Strange was pleased. He wanted to make Dormammu angry. "You gave Kaecilius powers from the Dark Dimension. I have special power from my world," he shouted. He lifted his left arm, and showed Dormammu the shining, green circles around it. "This is a time loop. It will never end."

Dormammu's great hand came down on him.

"Dormammu, I've come to bargain."

"You can't continue doing this," Dormammu shouted angrily.

"Yes, I can," said Strange.

"Then you will die, again and again."

"Yes," said Strange. In his head, he heard the Ancient One's words. *It's not about you.* "But everyone on Earth will live."

"But *you* will *suffer*," said Dormammu.

"Pain's an old friend," Strange said.

Dormammu's energy killed him again.

Dormammu killed Strange three more times. Then ...

"You will never win," Dormammu said.

"No." Strange knew that Dormammu was right. "But I can lose again and again and again and again."

He stood up. The pain was terrible. But he knew that he was doing the right thing.

"And you are my prisoner," he said.

"No! Stop! This must stop!" Dormammu shouted.

Ah, Strange thought. "No. I've come to bargain."

Dormammu moved close to him, and Strange could feel the heat of his anger.

"What do you want?" Dormammu asked.

At last, Strange thought. "Take your Zealots from my world. Stop attacking it. Never come back. If you do this, I'll break the loop."

"This is a time loop. It will never end."

"I Made a Bargain."

"Get up and fight, Strange!" Mordo said. "We will finish this."

Kaecilius and his Zealots walked toward him and Wong. Around them, nobody moved. Kaecilius looked at the sky. The energies of the Dark Dimension were moving there.

"Isn't it beautiful? A world without time. Without death."

Doctor Strange came down to the ground behind Kaecilius. He was returning at exactly the same time that he left. Mordo's mouth fell open in surprise.

Kaecilius turned around. "What have you done?" he asked.

"I made a bargain," said Strange.

Kaecilius looked down at his hands. The skin was becoming gray.

"What is this?" he asked, looking scared.

"Well, it's ... it's everything you wanted," Strange said. "Life without death as part of the One." Mordo and Wong came to stand next to him. Strange smiled. "You're not going to like it."

The bodies of Kaecilius and the Zealots began to move strangely. Their clothes started to burn. They lifted up in the air, and were pulled up, high into the sky. They disappeared into the Dark Dimension.

"He needed to steal the complete book," Strange said. "The part about the dangers of the spells comes *after* the spells."

He put his hands in front of him, and made the Eye's powerful, green circle. He turned it to the right. The three men looked around. Everywhere, people started moving again. They visited stores and continued their meals. They—and everyone on Earth—were safe now.

"We did it," Wong said.

Mordo looked very serious. "Yes. Yes, we did it. But we went against the natural laws."

"Look around you," Strange said. "It's finished. We saved the world from Dormammu."

"But we will pay for this," said Mordo. He didn't believe in the Ancient One now. Strange could see that he felt sad and hurt. "She went against our rules, and now we've done the same. We will pay. This is the end for me. I will leave this path."

Mordo turned and walked away. Strange and Wong watched him go.

Strange walked into the library at Kamar-Taj. The room was clean, and everything was in its place. *The students and sorcerers here have worked hard*, he thought.

The Eye of Agamotto hung on his chest. He knew that he must put it back in its place. He couldn't keep it. He moved his hands toward it, then stopped. With this kind of power ...

The Cloak of Levitation lifted off his shoulders and moved away.

"O.K." Strange said. He understood the message. He put the Eye back—it shone green.

Wong walked toward him.

"That was wise," he said. "You'll wear the Eye of Agamotto when you can use *all* its powers. But until then, you shouldn't walk in the streets with it. You're a great sorcerer. But you still have a lot to learn. The universe will learn about the Ancient One's death. There's no Ancient One to defend the Earth now. We must be ready."

Strange thought about all the people in the world. He could save them all.

"We'll be ready," he said.

The Cloak of Levitation dropped over his shoulders. Wong opened the door to the New York Sanctum, and the two men went through it. Strange walked up the main stairs of the Sanctum to a large window and put his watch on his wrist. The glass was still broken. He looked at his hand—it still shook. Then he stood up very straight. There was a lot to do.

Strange walked up the main stairs of the Sanctum to a large window and put his watch on his wrist.

Activities

Prologue & Chapter 1

Before you read

1 Discuss the picture of Doctor Strange on the Contents page.

   a Describe his appearance.
   b What do you think he is doing and feeling?

2 Look at the Word List at the back of the book. Check the meanings of new words in your dictionary. Then answer these questions.

   a What does a *sorcerer* do? What does a *surgeon* do? Use words from the Word List in your answers.
   b Is a *master* of *martial arts* good at martial arts? Can you give an example of a martial art?
   c What kind of *weapon* can *damage* a car?
   d Is it possible to *fold* a *robe*?
   e Who is a *powerful* person in your country?

3 Read In This Story and the Introduction. Discuss these questions.

   a What kind of person is Dr. Stephen Strange at the start of the story? How will he change, do you think?
   b Who is Christine Palmer? What will happen between her and Strange, do you think?
   c What will change Strange's life? What will he do because of this?
   d Who will Strange meet at the Sanctum in Kamar-Taj? Say a little about each person.
   e How will Strange change in Kamar-Taj? What will he learn?

While you read

4 Are these sentences right (✔) or wrong (✘)?

   a Kaecilius kills the librarian and sorcerers in the library. ◯
   b Kaecilius takes pages from a book to damage it. ◯
   c The Mirror Dimension is a magical space. ◯
   d The woman in the yellow robe casts a spell that kills Kaecilius. ◯

e She doesn't want him to use the spell from the book. ◯
f Dr. Christine Palmer agrees to go to dinner with Strange. ◯
g Strange has a car accident while looking at his phone. ◯
h The operation on Strange's hands is very successful. ◯
i Strange visits a man who learned to walk again. ◯

After you read

5   Prove that these statements are true. Give examples from the story.

a The woman in the yellow robe is a powerful sorcerer.
b Strange really wants to repair his hands.

6   How does Strange learn about Kamar-Taj? Why is he interested in it? Explain in your own words.

Chapters 2–3

Before you read

7   Discuss these questions. What do you think?

a How will Strange find Kamar-Taj?
b Why will Strange start to believe in magic?

While you read

8   Circle the incorrect word(s) in each of these sentences. Then write the correct word(s).

a Three men try to steal Strange's money.   ....
b The Ancient One is a man in a white robe.   ....
c The Ancient One says that a person's spirit can
repair his or her mind.   ....
d Mordo sends Strange into the Multiverse.   ....
e Mordo throws Strange out of a window.   ....

9   Write the speaker's name.

a "Open the door! Please!"   ....
b "Sorcerers called this language 'spells.'"   ....
c "That's *The Book of Cagliostro*. It's a book
about time."   ....

d "With sling rings, we can travel through the Multiverse."

e "Forget about yourself, Stephen."

10 Circle the correct sentence endings.

   a Strange goes into the library because he wants books on *astral projection / the Multiverse*.
   b Strange steals *the Eye of Agamotto / books*.
   c When things happen in the Mirror Dimension, *they don't change the real world / people in the real world can see them*.
   d Kaecilius stole a spell about *time / the Dark Dimension*.
   e Sorcerers protect the world from *Agamotto / mystical dangers*.
   f Dormammu wants to *destroy worlds / change time*.

After you read

11 Explain why these happen.

   a The Ancient One sends Strange into the Astral Dimension and the Multiverse.
   b Mordo throws Strange out of Kamar-Taj.
   c The Ancient One leaves Strange on a mountainside.
   d Strange cuts his hair and shaves his beard and mustache.

12 Discuss what you have learned about:

   the Ancient One   Kamar-Taj   the Multiverse
   relics   the Sanctums   Kaecilius   the Dark Dimension

   Do you believe that the Multiverse exists?

Chapters 4–6

Before you read

13 Discuss these questions.

   a Look at the last two sentences of Chapter 3: *The London portal opened. A man ran into the room and fell dead on the floor.* How do you think the man died? What will happen next?
   b In Chapter 4, Strange and Christine meet again. What will happen, do you think?

While you read

14 Answer these questions using one or two words.

   a Who casts a spell that damages Kamar-Taj? ....

   b Which city is Strange blown into? ....

   c Who does Kaecilius kill in the Sanctum? ....

   d What drops over Strange's shoulders? ....

   e Who does Kaecilius want to give the world to? ....

   f Who puts a Space Shard in Strange's chest? ....

15 Complete each sentence with one or two words.

   a Strange goes to his .... in New York for help.

   b He tells Christine that he needs an .... now.

   c He uses his .... to show her the right place in his chest.

   d His astral body fights with the astral body of a ....

   e He uses energy from a .... to win the fight in the hospital.

   f He tells Christine that he is .... about the past.

16 Are these sentences right (✔) or wrong (✗)?

   a All the Sanctums have fallen. ◯

   b Kaecilius is less powerful in the Mirror Dimension now. ◯

   c The Ancient One stops Kaecilius from killing Strange. ◯

   d The Ancient One takes power from the Dark Dimension. ◯

   e Kaecilius kills a Zealot and the Ancient One. ◯

17 Who is speaking, the Ancient One or Strange?

   a "What are you doing? You're dying!" ....

   b "It's not about you." ....

   c "I've hated taking power from the Dark Dimension." ....

   d "I'm not ready." ....

   e "I don't want you to go." ....

After you read

18 Discuss these questions.

   a What mistake does Strange make in these chapters?

   b What good things does he do?

   c Strange must choose between two possible futures. What are they?

   d What does he decide? How do we know?

   e What do we learn in the Ancient One's last conversation with Strange that are important to the story?

Chapters 7–8

Before you read

19 Look at these sentences from Chapters 7–8. What is going to happen, do you think?

    a "Dormammu is coming," Mordo said.
    b *I must make a time loop*, Strange thought.
    c "Dormammu!" Strange shouted. "I've come to bargain."

While you read

20 Complete each sentence with words on the right. Draw lines between them.

    a The Dark Dimension attacks   the Dark Dimension.
    b Strange casts a spell and time goes   Kamar-Taj.
    c Strange flies up into   Dormammu.
    d Strange bargains with   backward.
    e Kaecilius and the Zealots are taken into   Hong Kong.
    f Strange returns the Eye to   the Dark Dimension.

After you read

21 What happens in the Dark Dimension? Retell the story. Use these questions to help you:

    What does Strange do when he arrives in the Dark Dimension? What happens?
    How does he win against Dormammu? What is the result?

22 How do you think Strange feels at the end of the story? Where is he and why does he go there? What will he do next, do you think?

23 Work in groups of three. Kaecilius and the Zealots have disappeared into the Dark Dimension. Act out this conversation.

    Student A: You are Mordo. Say what you think and feel. Then leave.
    Student B: You are Strange. Talk about Kaecilius. Talk to Mordo. After he leaves, talk with Wong.
    Student C: You are Wong. Talk to Mordo. After he leaves, talk with Strange.

Writing

24 You are Christine. Write an email to your best friend after you operate on Strange. Describe what happened. Say how you feel.

25 You are Strange. You are in your room, and have a new, dark red robe. Write about your feelings on that day.

26 Write ten questions that you would like to ask the Ancient One before her death. Write her answers.

27 You are Strange at the end of the story. Write an email to Christine. Talk about the past and your feelings for her. Explain why you cannot spend much time with her now. Can you see a future life with her?

28 You are Wong after the end of the story. Write about each time that you were with Strange. Describe how your feelings about him changed.

29 You are Mordo. Write about the final fight in Hong Kong. Explain why you said, "I will leave this path."

30 Write a short report on the book. Describe what happens in one or two paragraphs. Give your opinion of the book, and the reasons for your opinion.

31 Write about your favorite person in the book. Explain why you like him/her.

32 You are going to make another movie about Doctor Strange. Which people from this story will be in it? Who will Strange fight, and why? What will happen? Will Strange use the Eye of Agamotto again?

Word List

astral projection (n) when someone's *spirit* is outside his/her body, in an astral body, and can travel to other places. An **astral body** looks like a person's real body, but most people cannot see it.

backward (adv) toward something behind you

bargain (n/v) an agreement with someone about something. In the agreement, each person gets something that he/she wants.

damage (n/v) when something is broken or badly hurt

dimension (n) one of the different parts of our reality. Our world has three dimensions of space, and one of time.

energy (n) something that makes movement possible. It also works machines. Electricity is a form of energy.

fold (v) to cover part of something with another part. This makes it smaller. You fold T-shirts before you put them away.

loop (n) a circle of something long and thin. In this book, a **time loop** is a *spell*. In a time loop, the same thing happens again and again.

magic (n) a special *power*. It can do things that don't seem possible.

martial arts (n) East Asian fighting skills. You usually fight with your hands and feet.

master (n) someone who has great skill at something. The Master can also be the most important person in an organization.

mystic (n/adj) someone who tries to understand other-worldly mysteries. The **mystic arts** are the use of different kinds of *magic*.

operate (on) (v) to cut into someone's body to repair it

portal (n) in this book, a *magical* entrance to another place

power (n) the ability—sometimes unnatural—to do something. A **powerful** person is very strong or important.

robe (n) a piece of clothing that looks like a long dress

sanctum (n) a special, private place—often in a religious building—that most people cannot go into

sorcerer (n) someone with *magical powers*

spell (n) words or actions that make *magic*. When you **cast a spell**, you make magic.

spin (v) to turn around again and again very fast

spirit (n) part of a person that is not the body. Some people believe that your spirit is the most important part of you.

surgeon (n) a hospital doctor who cuts into people's bodies

symbol (n) a sign, drawing, or thing that is used to mean something different

universe (n) all of space and time, and everything in it. In this book, the **Multiverse** is many different universes. Our universe is one of them. The Multiverse has no end.

weapon (n) something that you fight with, like a gun or a knife